MW01235635

THE SPIRITUAL MAN VERSUS THE CARNAL MAN

Anthony L. Mckoy

Be careful for nothing; but in everything by prayer and supplication with thanksgiving let your requests be made known unto God. **Philippians 4:6**

The Spiritual Man Versus The Carnal Man
by Anthony L. McKoy

Printed in the United States of America

ISBN 9781613797365

Unless otherwise indicated, Bible quotations are taken from The King James Version of the Bible.

Email address: a_mckoy@minister.com

www.xulonpress.com

To: Rev LAWRENCE phiri

mAy GoD Bless you in all
you do. Enjoy.

Andy P. mc_____
2016

PREFACE

I n this book, you will learn how to get victory over the flesh and the carnal mind. God has given us every weapon and tool we need to win the battle. The weapon is the Word of God, through the agent of the Holy Ghost.

As a believer, you must learn how to live and walk in the Spirit and knowledge of Jesus Christ. The only way Spirit filled children of

God can obtain victory is through the Word of God and the Spirit of the Lord. We are in a Spiritual war and we need to use Spiritual weapons in order to defeat, resist, and overcome the flesh, and have victory over temptation and the devil.

Therefore, it is important to do everything God says in His Word. Obedience to God's Word is the key to having victory over the flesh and the world. Victory builds faith and an overwhelming joy in your soul and spirit. What God has promised, He will bring it to pass.

Table of Content

Dedication

This book is dedicated to the late Rev. James L. Gilbert, who was my former Pastor, friend, and mentor in the Lord. His example of love and friendship will be greatly missed. His spirit will be cherished because he touched not only my life but other lives in so many ways with his love, his kindness, and his personality.

Rev. Gilbert never met a stranger. He talked with people whom he had just met as if he had known them for years. He loved everyone as if they were his own flesh and blood.

He had a hand in this book by encouraging me to finish what I started, and also by submitting the Foreword, which was so well written. I am grateful that I had a chance to meet him, and for him to be a part of my life.

My prayer is that someone will be blessed after reading this book, and that they may grow into the Spiritual man or woman that the Lord intends for them to be.

Special Thanks

First of all, I would like to thank my Lord and Savior Jesus Christ, for all He has done in my life, and for allowing this book to come to pass. Secondly, I would like to thank my wife, Laura Milton McKoy, for her love, patience, advisement, and humor, while writing this book.

Continual thanks to my parents John [deceased] and Mary McKoy, for raising me in the truth. Thank you to my Pastor Kevin

Wallace, for his guidance, support, and the leadership example he has shown. Thanks to my Pastor's wife, Crystal Wallace for taking an interest in and assisting with final editing, proofreading and the hours spent on this book.

Others I give thanks to are: my niece, Brandi Milton for typing, my sister-in-law Alicia Milton, my instructor at CCCC, Yukia Smiley and Arisha Foster for their editing. Also to my Mother-in-law, Mary Milton, for all her love and support, and Barbara Bryant for her persistent encouragement to write this book in its entirety.

Thanks to Rachelle Hypolite for the assistance in layout of this book cover. To my special friends, Nigel and Cleopatra Hinds, for their Christ-like spirit of love and sacrifice on the behalf of this book. I say "thank you" for everything.

To my church family of the Jacksonville First United Pentecostal Church, for your love and support for me and my wife, we say thank you for your unselfish generosity towards us, and believing that we would press on. Words cannot express our gratitude for all you have done. May God bless you in a great way.

Thank you!

FOREWORD
By the late Rev. James L. Gilbert

In the seventh chapter of this book, Anthony McKoy has touched the key-note that is accomplished in the works of the Kingdom of God. He has pointed out the nature of carnality, and he has shown us how the flesh and devil exploits our own human nature with things that the carnal man loves. However, Anthony McKoy also points out the motives of the Spiritual minded man, who uses the Spirit of God and the Word of God through the agency of the Holy Ghost to cultivate a desire to please God in everything.

He has very carefully shown us what the Holy Ghost desires in us, and what it means to be armed with the Sword of Spirit, which is the Word of God. The purpose of Brother McKoy writing on this subject is that we all may become prayer warriors and begin to fast and pray and intercede for the lost millions who walk after the flesh and not the Spirit. Prayer is a school we never finish with, because we can always learn more about it. We can learn from reading, but reading alone is not sufficient. We must practice as we read.

Prayer is like music; it is the keynote that brings harmony into our lives. As a friend and mentor to Brother McKoy, I want to add to this foreword the idea of prayer, not just the sincere desire of the heart, but actually getting into the spirit of prayer and verbalizing from the heart a communication that is so intense that it is as it were suspending us, between earth and heaven, and we actually lose ourselves in the presence of God, in so much that all carnal things are torn from us and we, for the time being are in perfect harmony with Jesus Christ.

First, prayer is an up-look; that is, it involves itself with praise and adoration. Then there is an in-look where we see personal needs and we make petitions in our own behalf. Then there is an outlook where we intercede for our fellow man. Before we need something done for us, we need something done to us. That is our greatest need. This is the element of prayer that is referred to in the word, men ought to always pray and not faint (Luke 18:1) and to pray without ceasing (Thessalonians 5:17). This means to stay in constant communication with God.

Brother McKoy has touched a sacred chord

in this discourse.

Chapter 1

The Nature of the Carnal Man

The carnal mind and the fleshly mind are one and the same. This is the nature that we inherited at birth, thanks to our fore-parents Adam and Eve. The only way we can battle this old sinful nature is through the new birth.

The Bible says in *St. John 3:3,* "Jesus answered and said unto him, Verily, verily, I say unto thee, Except a man be born again,

he cannot see the kingdom of God." Without

the new birth, we cannot discern Spiritual

things because they are spiritually discerned.

Paul talks about the carnality of the old man,

the old nature we were born with, and how

it must be dealt with. The Bible plainly states

that to the carnal mind spiritual things are

foolish. So if it is foolish, why put faith in it? It

does not make any sense to the person that

has not been born again. Listen to the words

of Jesus:

St. John 6: 44 "No man can come to me, except the Father which hath sent me draw him: and I will raise him up at the last day."

I Corinthians 2:14 "But the natural man receiveth not the things of the Spirit of God: for they are foolishness unto him: neither can he know them, because they are spiritually discerned."

The carnal mind is so out of touch with the things of God that it is like night and day. The natural mind is dead. Something that is dead cannot comprehend what is true and right, because it comes from God, through His spirit which He hath given us. The new birth is the only way that you and I can begin to understand God. In order for you to be victorious over the flesh, it takes the Spirit of God, and it must have pre-eminence over your life. Let us see what the word of God has to say about the carnality that is in your flesh:

Romans 7: 7-25

[7] What shall we say then? Is the law sin? God forbid. Nay, I had not known sin, but by the law: for I had not known lust, except the law had said, Thou shalt not covet.

[8] But sin, taking occasion by the commandment, wrought in me all manner of concupiscence. For without the law sin was dead.

[9] For I was alive without the law once: but when the commandment came, sin revived, and I died.

[10] And the commandment, which was ordained to life, I found to be unto death.

[11] For sin, taking occasion by the commandment, deceived me, and by it slew me.

[12] Wherefore the law is holy, and the commandment holy, and just, and good.

[13] Was then that which is good made death unto me? God forbid. But sin, that it might appear sin, working death in me by that which is good; that sin by the commandment might become exceeding sinful.

[14] For we know that the law is spiritual: but I am carnal, sold under sin.

[In these eight verses, Paul is writing concerning the law that deals with the flesh. The Jews could not keep the law, and neither can we Gentiles who have been adopted into God's covenant He made to Abraham. No matter how hard you try, you cannot live free from sin in the power of the flesh. It can only be done through the work of the Holy Ghost.]

[15] For that which I do I allow not: for what I would, that do I not; but what I hate, that I do.

[16] If then I do that which I would not, I consent unto the law that it is good.

[17] Now then it is no more I that do it, but sin that dwelleth in me.

[18] For I know that in me (that is, in my flesh,) dwelleth no good thing: for to will is present with me; but how to perform that which is good I find not.

[19] For the good that I would I do not: but the evil which I would not, that I do.

[20] Now if I do that I would not; it is no more I that do it, but sin that dwelleth in me.

[21] I find then a law, that, when I would do good, evil is present with me.

[22] For I delight in the law of God after the inward man:

[23] But I see another law in my members, warring against the law of my mind, and

bringing me into captivity to the law of sin which is in my members.

[When you attempt to live this Christian life by your own strength, you end up back at square one, which is through your sinful flesh. The good that you do is as filthy rags in the sight of God. You must totally depend on Jesus Christ, and not the power of the flesh.]

[24] O wretched man that I am! who shall deliver me from the body of this death?

[25] I thank God through Jesus Christ our Lord. So then with the mind I myself serve the law of God; but with the flesh the law of sin.

So we see according to scripture, the flesh cannot please God; it does not have the power or the will to do so. The work of God can only be done through faith and in the power of the Spirit of God. Paul had a struggle between his flesh wanting to do what it wanted to do, and the spirit wanting him to obey the Lord.

The nature of the flesh cannot, and will not, obey the word of God; it is not in his nature to do so. There is a war going on, and the battle is won or lost in the mind. Your spirit wants to obey God, but the flesh has a mind of its own. It all starts with the mind, so we must continually guard our thoughts. That is the only way to control your actions.

The devil has three ways that he attacks us according to *I John 2:16,* the lust of the flesh, the lust of the eyes, and the pride of life. These are the three main avenues in which temptation comes. In the Garden of Eden, the devil approached Eve through the lust of the flesh, the lust of the eyes, and the pride of life, telling her she would be as gods, knowing good and evil. Let us look at the scripture concerning the temptation in the Garden.

Genesis 3:1-6

[1]Now the serpent was more subtil than any beast of the field which the Lord God had made. And he said unto the woman, Yea hath God said Ye shall not eat of every tree of the garden?

[Notice which creature Satan chose to use; something that was similar to his character. The serpent was clever, cunning, intelligent, and beautiful, as Satan was when he was in heaven (Ezekiel 28:1-19). There could be several reasons why the devil came to Eve and not Adam. One could be that he detected that Eve was Adam's weakness. The Bible does not give a time frame of how long Adam and Eve were in the garden before Satan approached Eve with his lies. I believe he watched and observed them and saw that Adam really loved his wife. Maybe he felt like his wife was his way in because love seeks to please. Here are a few examples: Samson loved Delilah so much that he allowed her to seduce him into revealing where the secret of his strength lie. Also, Solomon loved and married many strange women, which led to his disobedience to God's law.

So we see that Satan came to Eve and injected doubt into her mind. When God gave Adam the commandment concerning the forbidden tree, Eve was not yet created. The devil realized she had second hand information, and therefore, there was room for doubt. His approach worked. The seed was planted and the rest is history.]

[2] And the woman said unto the serpent, we may eat of the fruit of the trees of the garden:

[3] But of the fruit of the tree which is in the midst of the garden, God hath said, Ye shall not eat of it, neither shall ye touch it, lest ye die.

[Notice she misquoted what God said. He did not use the word "touch," but Eve did. Information usually gets changed when being passed from one person to the next. The devil took advantage of that.]

[4] And the serpent said unto the woman Ye shall not surely die.

[You cannot afford to hold a conversation with the devil; you will be deceived every time. You must quote the word of God to him, and nothing less.]

[5] For God doth know that in the day ye eat thereof, then your eyes shall be opened, and ye shall be as gods, knowing good and evil.

[6] And when the woman saw that the tree was good for food, and that it was pleasant

to the eyes, and a tree to be desired to make one wise, she took of the fruit thereof, and did eat, and gave also unto her husband with her; and he did eat.

[Here is where the lust of the flesh entered in. One will give into fleshly desires if they are thought on long enough. Next, the lust of the eyes come into play. What the eyes see, they want. Finally, we have the pride of life. Everyone wants to be wise, he wanted her to believe that she would be like God. Satan tried that when he was in heaven and he was unsuccessful. Self deception can be the worst type of deception, if you are not careful.] Isaiah 14:12-17

Temptation will be here as long as the devil is around. He has to tempt you through one or all three of these, in order to accomplish his plan. Now let us move to the life of Jesus, and his temptation in the wilderness.

St. Matthew 4:1-11

[1] Then was Jesus led up of the Spirit into the wilderness to be tempted of the devil.

[2] And when he had fasted forty days and forty nights, he was afterward an hungered.

[3] And when the tempter came to him, he said, If thou be the son of God, command that these stones be made bread.

[4] But he answered and said, It is written, Man shall not live by bread alone, but by every word that proceedeth out of the mouth of God.

[First of all Jesus was led by the spirit of God into the wilderness to be tempted of the devil. He was not led by the flesh. When you are lead by the will or desires of the flesh, you will fail the test every time. Self-glorification can be your motive because you are trying to defeat a spirit in the flesh and it cannot be done, and no flesh will glory in His presence. Jesus was hungry, having not eaten in forty days. His flesh was weak. He also desired food. There is nothing wrong with eating. The problem is the manner in which we obtain what we want or need. It is the lust of the flesh that get us into trouble. Many people are guilty of abusing their power and position for personal gain. Satan used the words, "If thou be the son of God." He tried to make Jesus doubt who He was but Jesus knew perfectly well who He was. You must know who you are in Christ.]

[5] Then the devil taketh him up into the holy city, and setteth him on a pinnacle of the temple,

[6] And saith unto him, If thou be the Son of God, cast thyself down: for it is written, He shall give his angels charge concerning thee: and in their hands they shall bear thee up, lest at any time thou dash thy foot against a stone.

[7] Jesus said unto him, It is written again, Thou shalt not tempt the Lord thy God.

[This temptation deals with the pride of life. If Jesus would have cast Himself down and the angels had caught Him, the people would have known that He was whom He was saying He was. In other words, the devil was telling Him to prove that He really was Jesus. Jesus quoted the word to him, and so must you.]

[8] Again, the devil taketh him up into an exceeding high mountain, and sheweth him all the kingdoms of the world, and the glory of them;

[9] And saith unto him, all these things will I give thee, if thou wilt fall down and worship me.

[10] Then saith Jesus unto him, Get thee hence, Satan: for it is written, Thou shalt worship the Lord thy God, and him only shalt thou serve.

[11] Then the angels came and ministered unto him.

Now we come to the lust of the eyes.

Satan showed Jesus riches and kingdoms of

the world, but He offered Jesus something

He already owned. God has already promised to bless you in this life and in the life to come.

The devil came to Jesus the same way he came to Eve; through the flesh for food. When you are hungry, it is easy to give into temptation if you are not aware of what is happening.

St. Matthew 26: 41 "Watch and pray, that ye enter not into temptation: the spirit indeed is willing, but the flesh is weak."

The flesh is always weak when it comes to satisfying himself. Strength to resist temptation comes through the Spirit, not through the flesh, and the Bible tells us not to put confidence in the flesh.

Romans 8:1 tells us how to stay free from sin: "There is therefore now no condemnation to them which are in Christ Jesus, who walk not after the flesh, but after the Spirit." Walking in the Spirit gives you power to overcome the flesh. A person can have the Holy Ghost (the Spirit), but choose not to walk in the Spirit.

We must learn to walk in the Spirit in order to have victory over the flesh. We must be willing to suffer and deny the flesh in order to have victory. If we suffer in the flesh, we shall cease from sin. **Romans 8:8** "So then they that are in the flesh cannot please God." God desires for you to please Him and it can only come through a made up mind that you must live in the Spirit and not the flesh. It is not by might nor by power, but by His Spirit. Victory will come when you allow God to work through you, to the point that it is no more you, but Christ that lives in you. When you were born again, the old nature began to die, but dying is a daily process. When living in the Spirit becomes a way of life, then God can get the glory out of your life. The flesh and the Spirit are constantly in a struggle for control but the choice is yours. Ever since Adam and Eve fell in the Garden, there has always been fighting and wars, even until this day. Cain hated his brother Abel, for no reason, so he rose up and slew him. Jacob and Esau struggled in the womb. King Saul was jealous over David for many years, and tried to kill him on several occasions.

Today we still struggle with our flesh to do what is right. There is a war raging within us; the flesh wars against the Spirit. Jesus won the battle at Calvary but each must carry one's own cross. The only way to win our own personal battle is in, and through the Spirit.

Galatians 5: 16-18

[16] This I say then, Walk in the Spirit, and ye shall not fulfill the lust of the flesh.

[17]For the flesh lusteth against the Spirit, and the Spirit against the flesh: and these are contrary the one to the other: so that ye cannot do the things that ye would.

[18]But if ye are led of the Spirit, ye are not under the law.

The more you deny the flesh of its pleasures, the more liberty you have to become more like Jesus Christ. Just as He had to die in His physical body, so you must die to the old man, and his nature. You cannot live the Christian life in the old fallen nature because it is not subject to the law of God.

I Corinthians 15: 42-50

[42] So also is the resurrection of the dead. It is sown in corruption; it is raised in corruption:

[43] It is sown in dishonor; it is raised in glory: it is sown in weakness; it is raised in power:

[44] It is sown a natural body; it is raised a spiritual body. There is a natural body, and there is a spiritual body.

[45] And so it is written, the first man Adam was a living soul; the last Adam was made a quickening spirit.

[46] Howbeit that was not first which is spiritual, but that which is natural; and afterward that which is spiritual.

[47] The first man is of the earth, earthy: the second man is the Lord from heaven.

[48] As is the earthy, such are they also that are earthy: and as is the heavenly, such are they also that are heavenly.

[49] And as we have borne the image of the earthy, we shall also bear the image of the heavenly.

[50] Now this I say, brethren, that flesh and blood cannot inherit the kingdom of God; neither doth corruption inherit incorruption.

Trying to do the work of the Spirit in the power of the flesh cannot be done. God has given us the tools we need to be victorious. As Zechariah 4:6 put it, "not by power, nor by might, but by my Spirit saith the Lord." There will be times when you struggle in your flesh, which is in constant conflict with the spirit man.

I am reminded of Jesus right before His crucifixion. He was praying in the Garden of

Gethsemane. *St. Luke 22: 42* "Saying, Father, if thou be willing, remove this cup from me: nevertheless not my will, but thine, be done." His will was subject to the will of His Father. That is what you call total submission. Without total submission, God is not pleased with you. Partial obedience is not obedience when it comes to the word of God. The Lord will be your helper, if you seek him. *Hebrews 11: 6* "But without faith it is impossible to please him." The flesh cannot please or obey God. It cannot produce obedience or faith. Faith is produced by the Spirit, and the word of God. No matter how hard a person tries to obey God's law, it cannot be done outside of the way God has prescribed. You cannot live godly apart from the word of God, nor can you be successful in the power of your own strength.

Romans 3:10-12

[10] As it is written, There is none righteous, no, not one:

[11] There is none that understandeth, there is none that seeketh after God.

[12] They are all gone out of the way. They are together become unprofitable; there is none that doeth good, no, not one.

You do not have the power nor the ability to do the will of God on your own. When you go about to establish your own righteous-ness, it is all in vain.

Psalms 127: 1 "Except the Lord build the house, they labour in vain that build it: except the Lord keep the city, the watchman waketh but in vain."

Jesus Christ is the one that is making you into what He wants you to be. You cannot build your own spiritual house. You must rely on Him to do the work that must be done because according to scripture, Jesus is the builder.

St. Matthew 16: 18 "And I say also unto thee, That thou art Peter, and upon this rock

I will build my church; and the gates of hell shall not prevail against it."

No matter how the enemy comes against you, he cannot overcome you. All the wiles and tricks he may use, if you keep yourself in the word of God, he cannot break through God's protection. You are covered by the blood of Jesus Christ. You have all God's weapons at your disposal, to defeat the enemy.

Chapter 2

The Flesh and the Devil

The flesh and the devil are like hand and glove; they feed off one another. In order for the devil to get to you, he has to come through your mind; although he attacks other areas such as your body with sickness, your finances, and your family. It is all part of his plan to get control of your mind.

James 1:13-15

[13] Let no man say when he is tempted, I am tempted of God: For God cannot be tempted with evil, neither tempteth he any man:

[14] But every man is tempted, when he is drawn away of his own lust, and enticed.

[15] Then when lust hath conceived, it bringeth forth sin: and sin, when it is finished, bringeth forth death."

So whatever the adversary brings to you, it is always against the Word of God. We are all tempted but it cannot overtake us unless we allow it to.

I Corinthians 10:13 "There hath no temptation taken you but such as is common to man: but God is faithful, who will not suffer you to be tempted above that ye are able;

but will with the temptation also make a way of escape, that ye may be able to bear it."

The Lord has a purpose in the temptation. You may not understand everything that happens to you, but God has a plan in that particular trial that you may be experiencing from time to time. You must be aware of the enemy that is out to destroy you.

I Peter 5:8 "Be sober, be vigilant; because your adversary the devil, as a roaring lion walketh about, seeking whom he may devour." Satan's goal is to steal the word of God right out of your heart. He knows that the word is what brings faith into your heart and life. Your faith grows by exercising it.

Hearing the preached word of God will enrich

your spiritual life if you obey what you hear.

Romans 10:13-17

[13] For whosoever shall call upon the name of the Lord shall be saved.

[14] How then shall they call on him in whom they have not believed? And how shall they believe in him of whom they have not heard? And how shall they hear without a preacher?

[15] And how shall they preach, except they be sent? As it is written, How beautiful are the feet of them that preach the gospel of peace, and bring glad tidings of good things!

[16] But they have not obeyed the gospel. For Esaias saith, Lord who hath believed our report?

[17] So then faith cometh by hearing, and hearing by the word of God.

Hearing the word of God is the main thing that must take place if you want to have faith, and obeying the word is how your faith grows. The devil's goal is to cause you to be careless with the word that was given to you.

St. Mark 4:3-20

[3] Hearken; Behold, there went out a sower to sow:

[4] And it came to pass, as he sowed, some fell by the way side, and the fowls of the air came and devoured it up.

[5] And some fell on stony ground, where it had not much earth; and immediately it sprung up, because it had no depth of earth:

[6] But when the sun was up, it was scorched; and because it had no root, it withered away.

[7] And some fell among thorns, and the thorns grew up, and choked it, and it yielded no fruit.

[8] And other fell on good ground, and did yield fruit that sprang up and increased; and brought forth, some thirty, and some sixty, and some an hundred.

[9] And he said unto them, He that hath ears to hear, let him hear.

[10] And when he was alone, they that were about him with the twelve asked of him the parable.

[11] And he said unto them, unto you it is given to know the mystery of the kingdom of God: but unto them that are without, all these things are done in parables:

[12] That seeing you may see, and not perceive; and hearing they may hear, and not understand; lest at any time they should be converted, and their sins should be forgiven them.

[13] And he said unto them, Know ye not this parable? And how then will ye know all parables?

[14] The sower soweth the word.

[15] And these are they by the way side, where the word is sown; but when they have heard, Satan cometh immediately, and taketh away the word that was sown in their hearts.

[16] And these are they likewise which are sown on stony ground; who, when they have heard the word, immediately receive it with gladness;

[17] And have no root in themselves, and so endure but for a time: afterward, when affliction or persecution ariseth for the word's sake, immediately they are offended.

[18] And these are they which are sown among thorns; such as hear the word,

[19] And the cares of this world, and the deceitfulness of riches, and the lust of other things entering in, choke the word, and it becometh unfruitful.

[20] And these are they which are sown on good ground; such as hear the word, and receive it, and bring forth fruit, some thirty-fold, some sixty, and some an hundred.

What Jesus was trying to point out to his disciples is that the word of God must be your number one priority. You must guard your heart from the enemy. He comes as a thief, to steal, kill and to destroy. Guard it as though it were gold or silver. Your heart is the ground in which the word is sown, and there are certain things you must do in order to have a good harvest.

I remember when I was a child, my parents always planted a garden. We had to go out at least twice a week and pull up weeds we did not plant. The weeds were already in the ground with the seed, so when the plant would grow, the weeds would grow right along with the plant. If we did not pull up the weeds, they would choke the plants, and we would not have a good harvest.

We also had to water the garden every two or three days if there was no rain. We also had to sprinkle seven dust on the garden to protect it from insects. It is work when you want a fruitful harvest. Spiritually it is no different. It requires work to get the word of God rooted and grounded in your heart, that you may produce fruit. David declared in *Psalms 119: 11* "Thy word have I hid in mine heart, that I might not sin against thee." You must not allow yourself to get side tracked by the cares of this life, and therefore, lose out on eternal life.

You cannot listen to God and the devil at the same time. As soon as a thought comes to your mind and you know it is not of God, you must resist it right away. If not, it will take root in your heart and in just a matter of time, it will manifest itself. You cannot play with the devil in his ball park because you will never win. Unfortunately, many have tried it. Samson tried to play with the devil at his own game and he lost. The only way we can defeat temptation is do it God's way. Satan is the master of deception. He is very knowledgeable in the word, and also of man's weaknesses.

If he deceived one third of God's Holy angels into following him into trying to over-throw God in Heaven, what chance do you think you have outside of God's law? Angels are a lot more intelligent than you are. Human reasoning is no match for a spirit. You must rely on the word of God. Your enemy is very patient. He waits as long as it takes for the right moment, and then he strikes. If you are caught sleeping, you may become a casualty of war. We must be willing to suffer in order to avoid sin. He that hath suffered in the flesh hath ceased from sin. Suffering is a must. We either deny the Lord, or we deny ourselves; we cannot serve God and self.

Jesus put it another way: *St. Matthew 6:24* "No man can serve two masters: for either he will hate the one, and love the other; or else he will hold to the one, and despise the other; ye cannot serve God and mammon." Whoever you spend the most time with and whoever you feed the most, that is who will grow; the flesh or the spirit man. The flesh must be crucified daily and the spirit man must be fed daily with the Word of God. When you meditate on the Word, it strengthens your spirit, and a man without spirit is whipped.

Since the battle belongs to God, then you have only one thing to do: step back and let God do the work through His Spirit. You must learn to yield yourself to Him and watch Him perform a miracle through you. The devil has to lure you into fighting your own battle, and that is a lost battle when the flesh takes over. He works through the desires of the flesh;

therefore, you must learn to give God control of your desires.

David says it well in **Psalms 37: 4-5**

[4] Delight thyself also in the Lord; and he shall give thee the desires of thine heart.

[5]Commit thy way unto the Lord; trust also in him; and he shall bring it to pass.

Trust and commitment go hand in hand: you cannot have one without the other. When you completely trust the Lord, the battle is already won. You may not understand what God is up to; your job is to trust Him to work on your behalf, and leave the results to Him.

Chapter 3

The Nature of the Spiritually Minded Man

First of all, to be spiritually minded, one must be saved. One must repent from his sins, be baptized in Jesus' name, and be filled with the Holy Ghost.

Acts 2: 37- 38

[37] Now when they heard this, they were pricked in their heart, and said unto Peter,

and to the rest of the apostles, Men and brethren, what shall we do?

[38] Then Peter said unto them, Repent, and be baptized every one of you in the name of Jesus Christ for the remission of sins, and ye shall receive the gift of the Holy Ghost.

This is the first step in becoming spiritually minded. One of the main attributes of a spiritually minded man is that he keeps the attitude of a repentant heart. The ultimate desire in a saved person is to avoid sin. Job was a man that feared God and stayed clear from sin.

Job 1:8 "And the Lord said unto Satan, hast thou considered my servant Job, that there is none like him in the earth, a perfect and an upright man, one that feareth God, and escheweth evil." Here we see God bragging on Job because he avoids any type of evil. The Bible says the fear of the Lord is to hate evil. When a child of God sins, he should feel some type of remorse over the sin. God will hear a person that is of a broken heart and has a contrite spirit. In other words, one who is deeply sorry for his sins. *Isaiah 57:15* "For thus saith the high and lofty One that inhabiteth eternity, whose name is Holy, I dwell in the high and holy place, with him also that is of a contrite and humble spirit and to revive the heart of the contrite ones."

Humility is one of the main fruits in the spiritually minded man or woman. If we are going to obey God's Word, "humility" is the way. A humble person will repent if he or she has fallen short of God's word. We cannot let a day go by without repenting. We will never live well enough in this flesh that we will not need to repent. We are not perfect yet, but still striving for perfection. We must repent on a daily basis. If the devil can make us feel like we have got it made, we are deceived. We will not be perfect until Jesus comes.

We must daily seek God's will. We must be aware that our old nature is fighting against our new nature. Therefore, we will make mistakes and miss the mark, and the mark is Jesus. Because of this, we must ask for God's forgiveness on a daily basis. *I John 1:9* "If we confess our sins, he is faithful and just to forgive us our sins, and to cleanse us from all unrighteousness.

The Lord will not hear our prayers if we do not repent. *Psalms 66:18* "If I regard iniquity in my heart, the Lord will not hear me." The Spirit will lead us to repent of sins we have committed. Sin separates us from God, and the only way we can come back into the right relationship with God, is by repenting.

No amount of money or good deeds or sacrifices can take the place of repenting. *I Samuel 15:22* "And Samuel said, Hath the Lord as great delight in burnt offerings and sacrifices, as in obeying the voice of the Lord? Behold, to obey is better than sacrifice, and to hearken than the fat of rams."

It is hard for a man or woman to say, "I am sorry," and mean it. The carnal man does not like to humble himself. That is why we must walk in the Spirit and not in the flesh. The spiritually minded man will humble himself when he is wrong, but a person full of pride will not humble himself. God keeps the proud afar off, and that is where they will stay unless they humble themselves before God.

Selfishness cannot be a part of your life if you want to grow spiritually. The nature of the spiritually minded man has one desire; that is to please God. He is always seeking to do good for all mankind. He thinks of other people more than himself. His mind is always looking for ways to help even his enemies through prayer and fasting.

Psalms 35:11-14 says,

[11] False witnesses did rise up; they laid to my charge things that I knew not.

[12] They rewarded me evil for good to the spoiling of my soul.

[13] But as for me, when they were sick, my clothing was sackcloth: I humbled myself with fasting; and my prayer returned into mine own bosom.

[14] I behaved myself as though he had been my friend or brother: I bowed down heavily, as one that mourneth for his mother.

Fasting brings the flesh under control so that you can seek after God with a sincere heart. It does not make you holy; the word of God is what causes you to become holy. It is very easy to become carnal if you are not watchful. From time to time you must push the plate back with fasting and prayer. Pick up your Bible and study it daily so that you can stay strong in the Lord. You eat food every day in order to grow and have a strong body, then you must eat God's word daily in order to stay spiritually strong.

You must guard your thoughts at all times because the enemy will plant wicked thoughts in your heart and mind, and cause you to become carnal. You may wake up one day and realize how far in left field you are. Repentance is the only way to get back. If you pray, you will stay; if you fast, you will last. If you do not pray, you will become *prey.* If you do not talk to God, you will talk to the devil. If you do not develop an intimate relation-ship with the Lord, you will become a casu-alty of war. Casual relationships do not last.

You must stay alert at all times in order to avoid the enemies attack.

It is in the Spirit that a person lives for God. One must walk in the Spirit so they will not fulfill the lust of the flesh. You must daily crucify the flesh and its desires in order to live for Jesus. *Galatians 2:20* "I am crucified with Christ: nevertheless, I live; yet not I, but Christ liveth in me: and the life which I now live in the flesh I live by the faith of the Son of God, who loved me, and gave himself for me." You live a crucified life in this body which belongs to the Lord. You live out the life of Jesus Christ in your body. You must completely surrender to the will of God. It is a daily death to the flesh, something that you do not always enjoy. No one wants to die; it is usually painful, yet fulfilling to the Spirit man. As was mentioned earlier, the Bible has scriptures in reference to the mind. A few are listed below that may help you win the mind battle.

Deuteronomy 18:6 "And if a Levite come from any of thy gates out of all Israel, where he sojourned, and come with all the desire of his (**mind**) unto the place which the Lord shall choose;"

I Chronicles 28:9 "And thou, Solomon my son, know thou the God of thy father, and serve him with a perfect heart and a willing (**mind**): for the Lord searcheth all hearts, and understandeth all the imaginations of the thoughts: if thou seek him, he will be found of thee; but if thou forsake him, he will cast thee off forever."

Isaiah 26:3 "Thou wilt keep him in perfect peace, whose (**mind**) is stayed on thee: because he trusteth in thee."

Nehemiah 4:6 "So built we the wall; and all the wall was joined together unto the half thereof: for the people had a (**mind**) to work."

Mark 5:15 "And they come to Jesus, and see him that was possessed with the devil, and had the legion, sitting, and clothed, and in his right (**mind**): and they were afraid."

Matthew 22:37 "Jesus said unto him, Thou shalt love the Lord thy God with all thy heart, and with all thy soul, and with all thy (**mind**)."

Acts 17:11 "These were more noble than those in Thessalonica, in that they received the word with all readiness of (**mind**), and searched the scriptures daily, whether those

things were so."

Romans 8:5-7

[7] For they that are after the flesh do (**mind**) the things of the flesh; but they that are after the Spirit the things of the Spirit.

[6] For to be carnally (**minded**) is death; but to be spiritually (**minded**) is life and peace.

[7] Because the carnal (**mind**) is enmity against God: for it is not subject to the law of God, neither indeed can be.

Romans 12:1, 2

[1] I beseech you therefore, brethren, by the mercies of God, that ye present your bodies a living sacrifice, holy, acceptable unto God, which is your reasonable service.

[2] And be not conformed to this world; but be ye transformed by the renewing of your (**mind**), that ye may prove what is that good, and acceptable, and perfect, will of God.

II Corinthians 8:12 "For if there be first a willing (**mind**), it is accepted according to that a man hath, and not according to that he hath not."

Ephesians 2:3 "Among whom also we all had our conversation in times past in the lusts of our flesh, fulfilling the desires of the flesh and of the (**mind**); and were by nature the children of wrath, even as others."

Philippians 2:5 "Let this (**mind**) be in you, which was also in Christ Jesus."

Colossians 2:18 "Let no man beguile you of your reward in a voluntary humility and worshipping of angels, intruding into those things which he hath not seen, vainly puffed up by his fleshly (**mind**)."

II Thessalonians 2:2 "That ye be not soon shaken in (**mind**), or be troubled, neither by spirit, nor by word, nor by letter as from us, as that the day of Christ is at hand."

II Timothy 1:7 "For God hath not given us the spirit of fear; but of power, and of love, and a sound (**mind**)."

I Peter 1:13 "Wherefore gird up the loins of your (**mind**), be sober and hope to the end for the grace that is to be brought unto you at the revelation of Jesus Christ."

Christians must be alert at all times.

St. Matthew 26:41 "Jesus said to watch and pray, that ye enter not into temptation: the spirit is indeed willing, but the flesh is weak." We cannot allow ourselves to get caught up in the world, and be guilty of ignoring the will of God.

II Timothy 2:1-4

[1] Thou therefore, my son, be strong in the grace that is in Christ Jesus.

[2] And the things that thou hast heard of me among many witnesses, the same commit thou to faithful men, who shall be able to teach others also.

[3] Thou therefore endure hardness, as a good soldier of Jesus Christ.

[4] No man that warreth entangleth himself with the affairs of this life; that he might

please him who hath chosen him to be a soldier.

As I stated in chapter 3, we are in a war and the enemy is out to take anything that is good and spiritual from our lives.

St. Luke 22:31, 32

[31] And the Lord said, Simon, Simon, behold Satan hath desired to have you, that he may sift you as wheat:

[32] But I have prayed for thee, that thy faith fall not: and when thou art converted, strengthen thy brethren.

I remember as a child growing up watching my mother make a cake from scratch. She would sift the flour into a bowl. Whatever was left in the sifter, was thrown in the trash. That is what the devil tries to do to you. He wants to sift all the good out, until there is nothing left but carnality. You must constantly pray, "Lord, keep my mind on you."

The cares of this life can sneak into your life unawares and choke out the word of God, keeping it from growing like it should. Jesus, speaking in *St. Luke 21:34-36,* said

[34] And take heed to yourselves, lest at any time your hearts be overcharged with surfeiting, and drunkenness, and cares of this life, and so that day come upon you unawares.

[35] For as a snare shall it come on all them that dwell on the face of the earth.

[36] Watch ye therefore, and pray always, that ye may be accounted worthy to escape all these things that shall come to pass, and to stand before the son of man.

When you stop watching, you stop praying. When you stop praying, you stop watching. Then you become prey to the devil. You cannot allow the enemy to lull you to sleep. When you are asleep, you have no idea what is going on around you. You cannot defend yourself if you are sleep, so you must stay alert at all times. The enemy will steal your protection, which is your weapon. If your weapon is gone, then you are easy prey. Fear sets in, and you have no sense of what to do. If you allow fear to control you God cannot work where fear is in control. In the physical army, you are in trouble, but in

God's army, all you can do is pray. You must do all that you can in order to stay alert to the enemy. Do not allow yourself to fall prey to the trap of carelessness. Many soldiers have died because of carelessness. Let your guard down, and he comes in like a flood and you will not have time to recover from your mistake, or his attack. You must call on the mercy of God.

CHAPTER 4

THE SPIRIT OF GOD AND THE WORD OF GOD

The Spirit and the Word go hand-in-glove. You cannot separate the two and be saved, because the spirit feeds and lives off of the Word of God. *St. John 1:1* tells us, "In the beginning was the Word, and the Word was with God, and the Word was God."

Without the Word, we would not know whether we are in God's will or not. The Word is our road map. The Word is our light; it is everything we need. *Hosea 4:6* "My people are destroyed for lack of knowledge." To know God's Word is to know God. The Spirit will lead and guide you into all truth if you study God's Word. The Word is like a seed. It must be planted and watered. The weeds are negative thoughts that must be pulled up and out. You must feed a plant as needed, if it is to grow and stay alive. The Word is Spiritual food. If you do not feed your spirit on a daily basis, it will not grow.

I Peter 2:2 tells us, "As newborn babes desire the sincere milk of the word that ye may grow thereby." It is impossible to grow without the Word. If you do not feed a new-born baby, it will die. If you do not feed a newborn spiritual babe, it will die. You must continuously feed on the Word to stay healthy and strong. The Spirit and the Word are one. God's Word is a must in this Christian life. You grow, live and die to the old nature by the Word. God's Word is God according to *St. John 1:1.* We know that God is a Spirit, and Jesus said that His words were Spirit, and they are life. Since we are in a spiritual war, we must know our enemy and we must know our weapons. The Word can be everything we need it to be, whenever we need it.

The Spirit uses the Word against the enemy.

In *St. Matthew 4:1-11,* Jesus used the Word

against the devil. We must be walking in the

power of the Spirit in order to use the Word.

The flesh will not, and cannot use the Word.

When God's Word goes forth, who can stop

it?

Isaiah 45: 23 tells us, "I have sworn by

myself, the word is gone out of my mouth

in righteousness, and shall not return, That

unto me every knee shall bow, every tongue

shall swear."

There is power in the Word of God. We, as saints of the Most High God, are given the privilege to use His Word for every situation that might come upon us. *Isaiah 54: 17* "No weapon that is formed against thee shall prosper; and every tongue that shall rise against thee in judgment thou shalt condemn. This is the heritage of the servants of the Lord, and their righteousness is of me, saith the Lord."

The Spirit and the Word together are like a hurricane with wind and water. They tear up and pull down everything that they come in contact with. The Word and the Spirit have all wisdom and power.

Exodus 31: 3 "And I have filled him with the Spirit of God, in wisdom and in understanding, and in knowledge and in all manner of workmanship."

We must be wise as serpents and harmless as doves to defeat the enemy. Wisdom gives you the ability to see afar off. It is impossible to defeat the enemy without wisdom. The devil has been around a long time and has a lot of experience in causing man to fall. ***Proverbs 3: 13*** "Happy is the man that findeth wisdom, and the man that getteth understanding." Wisdom leads us into the perfect will of God. Wisdom is stronger than weapons of war. Wisdom is like a light that shines in the darkest of trials and tests; you will be victorious in Jesus, if you stay in the word.

CHAPTER 5

THINGS THAT THE HOLY GHOST LOVES

The number one thing that our spirit loves is pleasing God. You must have a burning desire to please God in order to stay with God. Where there is no desire for God and things of God, a person will not stay with God. People do what they want to do. A love for God is a must to stay saved.

Galatians 5:22 tells us about the fruit of the Spirit. A person must produce fruit to stay alive in God. A tree that does not bear fruit is a dead tree or something is wrong with that tree. The root may be dead and if so, it cannot bring forth fruit. If we are rooted in the word of God, nothing, or nobody, can pluck us out of His hand. If one does not love the Word, then he or she ceases to grow in God. We eat what we love. What we do not like, we do not eat. But when it comes to God's Word, we must eat the whole roll. Whatever the Word says to do, we should find ourselves doing it, if we love God. The love for the Word of God will lead us to fast, pray, study and show love to others. We will deny ourselves and follow Christ. Fasting brings the flesh under subjection so that we can obey God. Fasting is a type of discipline or chastisement to the flesh, just like the rod is chastisement for a child. A person walking in the flesh cannot obey God. Fasting keeps us more spiritually minded so that we can walk in the Spirit, therefore, it should be part of our Spiritual walk with the Lord.

Prayer is another thing that the Holy Ghost loves. A person who does not pray is actually telling God they do not need Him. The person who thinks he does not need God is a fool. [Psalms 53:1] It is impossible to stay saved without prayer.

You cannot build a relationship with the Lord without prayer. Prayer is a powerful weapon against the enemy. The devil trembles when the weakest child of God prays. The Spirit loves the Word and the Word brings joy to your spirit.

According to **Nehemiah 8:10,** the joy of the Lord is your strength. The more joy you have, the better chance you have of defeating the enemy. Where there is joy, there is peace, because the Word brings peace. Peace is of

God. Where there is no peace, there is war. When you are in the Spirit of prayer, it keeps you watchful; it keeps your mind sober. When you learn to love the things of the Spirit, your faith will be increased and it will become a lot easier to serve God. You must learn to live in the Spirit of love that comes from the Holy Ghost. Without a burning love for God, the enemy will put your light out. A love for the Word will keep your light burning. Love brings light, and Jesus is the light of the world. Where the Spirit of the Lord is, there is light, and darkness leaves. That darkness is sin. A burning love for the Word will burn sin up. God's Word is a burning fire and fire purifies. *Malachi 3: 2, 3* "But who may abide the day of his coming? and who shall stand when he appeareth? for he is like a refiner's fire, and like fuller's soap: and he shall sit as a refiner and purifier of silver: and he shall purify the sons of Levi, and purge them as gold and silver, that they may offer unto the Lord an offering in righteousness." God filled you with the Holy Ghost and fire. The fire that comes with the Holy Ghost is what keeps you working and living for the Lord.

You cannot sit on a physical fire and not be burned. The spiritual life is the same. If you are sitting down on the Holy Ghost, that is a good sign that your fire has gone out, or is going out. God wants you to be either hot or cold. When the fire (of the Holy Ghost) goes out, sin comes in. You understand how natural heat works; when you turn the heat off in your home in the winter time, it gets cold. Or if you do not continue to put wood on the fire in the fireplace, the fire goes out. **Proverbs 26: 20** "Where no wood is, there the fire goeth out." Your spiritual heat is turned on by studying and obeying God's Word. Cold and heat cannot stay together. Light and darkness cannot stay together.

You must feed the Spiritual man the things that will help him stay in this Christian race. It makes no difference how fast or slow you may run, as long as you stay in the race.

Ecclesiastes 9:11 "I returned, and saw under the sun, that the race is not to the swift, nor the battle to the strong, neither yet bread to the wise, nor riches to men of understanding, nor yet favor to men of skill; but time and chance happeneth to them all."

The Holy Ghost is a Spirit which produces Spiritual fruit of love, joy, peace, longsuffering, gentleness, goodness, faith, meekness, and temperance. Fasting, prayer, studying the

Word, meditation, witnessing, and obeying the Word will help feed the root of your Spiritual tree, or the Spiritual man. Your Spirit must eat in order to survive and to do battle against the enemy of your soul.

The battle is won or lost in the mind. Just like feeding the physical body, what you feed your mind is just as important. The mind controls your actions, whether right or wrong, good or bad. Thoughts are seeds that produce whatever has been planted; therefore, you must be careful what you plant in your mind and heart. Your heart and mind are so vital to your spiritual growth. It is the center of your actions. **Proverbs 23:7** says: "As he thinketh in his heart so is he." Webster defines the word *think* "to have the mind occupied on some subject, to imagine, to consider, believing." Since you must think about something, it might as well be something good and righteous.

Philippians 4:6-8

[6]Be careful for nothing; but in everything by prayer and supplication with thanksgiving let your request be made known unto God.

[7] And the peace of God, which passeth all understanding, shall keep your heart and minds through Christ Jesus.

[8] Finally, brethren, whatsoever things are true, whatsoever things are honest, whatsoever things are just, whatsoever things are pure, whatsoever things are lovely, whatsoever things are of a good report; if there be

any virtue, and if there be any praise, think on these things.

God gets no glory out of carnal minded thoughts because you become what you think about. That is why you must be careful what you think. E. M. Bounds said it this way: "Sow a thought, you reap an act; sow an act, you reap a habit; sow a habit, you reap a character; sow a character, you reap your destiny." Your destiny should be aimed for heaven. God created heaven and earth, and mankind, but He had to think about it first. The mind is so powerful because we are created in His image.

God is concerned about what we think. His plan is to make us into the image of Jesus Christ. **Philippians 2:5** "Let this mind be in you, which was also in Christ Jesus." Jesus had a mind and heart to please the Father in everything. We cannot be half-hearted about what we do for the Lord. Your whole heart, soul, mind, and body must be into pleasing the Lord. The heart is the main ingredient in your obedience to God's law.

Jeremiah 17:9 "The heart is deceitful above all things, and desperately wicked: who can know it?" Everything surrounds the heart, and God judges a person's heart more than the outward appearance. You must be careful what you allow in your heart.

Proverbs 4:23 "Keep the heart with all diligence; for out of it are the issues of life."

Your heart is the key ingredient to living a fruitful life for the Lord Jesus Christ. You cannot partially serve God and live a victorious life. Your whole heart, soul, and mind must be involved in whatever you do.

Psalm 119:2 "Blessed are they that keep his testimonies, and that seek him with the whole heart."

Your whole heart must be completely given to God, in order to see a difference in your life. God judges the inward man.

CHAPTER 6

KNOWLEDGE OF THE SWORD
OF THE SPIRIT

Knowledge of your weapons is a must. You must know your weapon from top to bottom. Your Spiritual weapon is the Word of God. The Word is the Spirit's sword and every soldier needs a sword. Without a sword on the battlefield, you will not stay alive.

You must study your weapon daily because the enemy knows your weapon better than you do. He has been around a long time and he has caused great men of God to fall. If a person does not know God's Word, he will be defeated. The Word is what keeps you.

James 4:6-8

[6] But he giveth more grace. Wherefore he saith, God resisteth the proud, but giveth grace to the humble.

[7] Submit yourselves therefore to God. Resist the devil, and he will flee from you.

[8] Draw nigh to God, and he will draw nigh to you. Cleanse your hands, ye sinners: and purify your hearts, ye double minded.

You must resist the devil with God's Word.

There is no other weapon that can defeat

the adversary and the flesh other than God's Word. The Word is your only hope. Nothing can stand against this Word. One must have wisdom of the Word according to **Colossians 1:9, 10.** You must be filled with spiritual knowledge, wisdom and understanding in order to walk worthy of the Lord unto all pleasing being fruitful in every good work, and increasing in the knowledge of God. You must know the Word in order to stay alive, for a wise man listens to instructions. The devil is very intelligent. That is why you must be as wise as serpents, but harmless as doves.

Proverbs 4:7 "Wisdom is the principal thing; therefore get wisdom: and with all thy getting get understanding." A person that has the wisdom of God's Word can see the devil's traps. One must hate sin and fear the Lord in order to stay free from the enemy's devices. Job said in ***Job 28:28***, "And unto man he said, Behold, the fear of the Lord, that is wisdom; and to depart from evil is understanding." A man or woman will die if he or she does not learn the fear of the Lord. It is through the wisdom and understanding of God that you have victory in your walk with the Lord.

Paul's prayer for the Ephesians was that they might know the Lord in a greater way.

Ephesians 1: 15-19

[15] Wherefore I also, after I heard of your faith in the Lord Jesus, and love unto all the saints,

[16] Cease not to give thanks for you, making mention of you in my prayers;

[17] That the God of our Lord Jesus Christ, the Father of glory, may give unto you the spirit of wisdom and revelation in the knowledge of Him: [18] The eyes of your understanding being enlightened; that ye may know what is the hope of his calling, and what the riches of the glory of his inheritance in the saints,

[19] And what is the exceeding greatness of His power to us-ward who believe, according to the working of his mighty power.

There is so much God has in store for you, if you would only seek after Him with all your heart. He has equipped you with so much of His goodness that the enemy does not stand a chance to defeat you.

James 1: 5-8

[5] If any of you lack wisdom, let him ask of God, that giveth to all men liberally, and upbraideth not; and it shall be given him.

[6] But let him ask in faith, nothing wavering. For he that wavereth is like a wave of the sea driven with the wind and tossed.

[7] For let not that man think that he shall receive any thing of the Lord.

[8] A double minded man is unstable in all his ways.

God is willing to give you what you need to fight this battle and finish the job He has given you. It is going to take the wisdom of God that comes from His word in order to live a Godly life in this present world, and come out victorious in the end. There is a work that must be done and it is going to take wisdom, knowledge, and understanding to do it God's way. Concerning the building of the tabernacle, Moses had to choose men and women that were skilled in that area.

Exodus 35: 30-35

[30] And Moses said unto the children of Israel, See, the Lord hath called by name

Bezaleel the son of Uri, the son of Hur, of the tribe of Judah;

[31] And he hath filled him with the spirit of God, in wisdom, in understanding, and in knowledge, and in all manner of workmanship;

[32] And to devise curious works, to work in gold, and in silver, and in brass,

[33] And in the cutting of stones, to set them, and in carving of wood, to make any manner of cunning work.

[34] And he hath put in his heart that he may teach, both he, and Aholiab, the son of Ahisamach, of the tribe of Dan.

[35] Them hath he filled with wisdom of heart, to work all manner of work, of the engraver, and of the cunning workman, and of the embroiderer, in blue, and purple, in scarlet, and in fine linen, and of the weaver, even of them that do any work, and of those that devise cunning work.

There are many Biblical examples that show us how wisdom or knowledge played a major part in people's lives.

Acts 7: 9, 10

[9] And the patriarchs, moved with envy, sold Joseph into Egypt: but God was with him,

[10] And delivered him out of all his afflictions, and gave him favor and wisdom in the sight of Pharaoh king of Egypt; and he made him governor over Egypt and all his house.

Joseph had to have the wisdom of God to be the overseer in Potiphar's house. It took wisdom, and the fear of God, in order for Joseph to run from Potiphar's wife when she tried to seduce him into committing a sexual act that was wrong and sinful. It took wisdom and the favor of God when he was put in prison and God was with him and showed him the interpretation of dreams of other prison inmates. It took wisdom when he was called out of prison to interpret the Pharaoh's dream and he was made governor of the land of Egypt.

Acts 7: 22 "And Moses was learned in all the wisdom of the Egyptians, and was mighty in words and in deeds." While in Egypt, Moses had to learn the ways, customs, and culture in which he lived. Egypt would later become the enemy of Moses. You must do the same in this present world. The flesh, the

---

devil, and the world are your enemies. You must have the wisdom of God in your heart in order to combat these evil forces.

I Kings 4:29-31

[29] And God gave Solomon wisdom and understanding exceeding much, largeness of heart, even as the sand that is on the sea shore.

[30] And Solomon's wisdom excelled the wisdom of all the children of the east country, and all the wisdom of Egypt.

[31] For he was wiser than all men; than Ethan the Ezrahite, and Heman, and Chalcol, and Darda, the sons of Mahol: and his fame was in all nations round about.

Solomon knew he needed wisdom in order to lead the nation. God honored his request by giving him wisdom and riches. There was no other man like Solomon in the Old Testament becuase of this. If you want to be great for God, you need the wisdom of God.

There were four young men in captivity in Babylon, who stood out while in captivity because of their faith and their wisdom.

Daniel 1:17-20

[17] As these four children, God gave them knowledge and skill in all learning and wisdom: and Daniel had understanding in all visions and dreams.

[18] Now at the end of the days that the king had said he should bring them in, then the prince of the eunuchs brought them in before Nebuchadnezzar.

[19] And the king communed with them; and among them all was found none like Daniel, Hananiah, Mishael, and Azariah: there stood they before the king.

[20] And in all matters of wisdom and understanding that the king enquired of them he found them ten times better than all the magicians and astrologers that were in his entire realm.

Last but not least, Jesus was known for wisdom. *St. Luke 2:40* "And the child grew, and waxed strong in spirit, filled with wisdom: and the grace of God was upon him." Jesus surely needed the wisdom of God in order to deal with what He was about to encounter.

Isaiah 5:13 says that God's people go into captivity because they have no knowledge. You must educated in the word of God in order to live a successful Christian life.

Developing an intimate relationship with the Lord is so important in your walk with Him. You cannot truly love someone if you do not know them. Time must be spent with the Lord if you want to grow in faith. You will not get to know the fullness of God over night. You must be tried and proven in order to stay with God. When Jesus was tempted of the devil in the wilderness, listen to what words He used:

St. Matthew 4:4 "It is written, man shall not live by bread alone, but by every word that proceedeth out of the mouth of God."

When God said every word, He meant every word; not some of the word, but all of God's Word. You must know what is written in order to defeat the enemy. The devil has no fear of you if you do not know and believe the Word of God. You are a soldier in the army of the Lord so you must learn how to use the Word. You must search the scriptures daily to know what the Word says.

Acts 17:11 "These were nobler than those in Thessalonica, in that they received the word with all readiness of mind, and searched the scriptures daily, whether those things were so."

As a child of God, you must search God's Word for yourself, and not just take someone else's word. Know God for yourself. God will hold you responsible for searching His word. For example, it takes time for married couples to learn their new spouse. They must get to know their likes and dislikes. If a man knows his wife does not like blue, then he should not go and buy her a blue dress.

If a woman knows her husband does not like chicken, then why would she cook chicken for dinner? You must spend quality time with someone in order to get to know them; quality not quantity. It is the same way with your relationship with God. If you know that God hates sin, then you must purpose in your heart to stay away from sin. Love seeks to please. Paul had a desire to please the Lord and to please him in the fullness. He did not care what he had to give up or lose.

Philippians 3:7-10

[7] But what things were gain to me, those I counted loss for Christ.

[8] Yea doubtless, and I count all things but loss for the excellency of the knowledge of Christ Jesus my Lord: for whom I have suffered the loss of all things, and do count them but dung, that I may win Christ,

[9] And be found in him, not having mine own righteousness, which is of the law, but that which is through the faith of Christ, the righteousness which is of God by faith:

[10] That I may know him, and the power of his resurrection, and the fellowship of his sufferings, being made conformable unto his death.

You must have a desire to seek and to please the Lord at all cost. Knowing Him must be your number one goal. True joy comes from knowing who Jesus is. If you are going to boast or brag or glory in something, let it be in knowing the Lord.

Jeremiah 9:23, 24

[23] Thus saith the Lord, let not the wise man glory in his wisdom, neither let the mighty man glory in his might, let not the rich man glory in his riches:

[24] But let him that glorieth glory in this, that he understandeth and knoweth me, that I am the Lord which exercise lovingkindness, judgment, and righteousness, in the earth: for in these things I delight, saith the Lord.

Knowing Him causes your love to grow for Him. By loving Him, you seek to please and obey.

St. John 14:15 "If ye love me, keep my commandments." Love is the ingredient that constrains you to obey God's law. Whatever you do for the Lord or others, you should do out of love for the Lord. The more you love the Lord, the more you want to know him. You cannot serve God out of duty or tradition, but out of love.

The Pharisees were trying to keep the letter of the law, but the Spirit brings love and life. ***II Corinthians 3:2-6***

[2] Ye are our epistle written in our hearts, known and read of all men:

[3] Forasmuch as ye are manifestly declared to be the epistle of Christ ministered by us, written not with ink, but with the spirit of the living God; not in tables of stone, but in fleshly tables of the heart.

[4] And such trust have we through Christ to God-ward:

[5] Not that we are sufficient of ourselves to think anything as of ourselves: but our sufficiency is of God;

[6] Who also hath made us able ministers of the New Testament; not of the letter, but of the spirit: for the letter killeth, but the spirit giveth life.

The enemy will come and test your knowledge of the Bible, so you must know your weapon in order to pass the test. Your love for the Lord must be put on trial. You may think you will do this or that for the Lord, but the test will let you know. God already knows where you stand with him. The battle belongs to the Lord, but the victory is yours, if you will put your trust in Him. You should not fight a battle that belongs to the Lord. The flesh will take the credit for winning the battle. Therefore there is no true victory. You cannot win against the flesh nor evil spirits without the spirit of the Lord ruling in your life.

CHAPTER 7

THE SPIRITUAL ARMOUR
THAT IS NEEDED

Every soldier needs armour, and God has given us His Spiritual armour to fight the enemy, but we must put it on and use it properly to stay alive. Paul tells us about this armour and what pieces are to be worn.

We must wear every piece to be victorious.

Ephesians 6:10-20

[10] Finally, my brethren, be strong in the Lord, and in the power of his might.

[11] Put on the whole armour of God, that ye may be able to stand against the wiles of the devil.

[12] For we wrestle not against flesh and blood, but against principalities, against powers, against the rulers of the darkness of this world, against spiritual wickedness in high places."

[13] Wherefore take unto you the whole armour of God, that ye may be able to withstand in the evil day, and having done all, to stand.

[14] Stand therefore, having your loins girt about with truth, and having on the breastplate of righteousness;

[15] And your feet shod with the preparation of the gospel of peace;

[16] Above all, taking the shield of faith, wherewith ye shall be able to quench all the fiery darts of the wicked.

[17] And take the helmet of salvation, and the sword of the Spirit, which is the word of God:

[18] Praying always with all prayer and supplication in the Spirit, and watching thereunto with all perseverance and supplication for all saints;

[19] And for me, that utterance may be given unto me, that I may open my mouth boldly, to make known the mystery of the gospel,

[20] for which I am an ambassador in bonds: that therein I may speak boldly, as I ought to speak.

First of all, Paul encourages us to be strong in the Lord, and to put on every piece of armour God has provided. You are strong in the Spirit of the Lord, and not the flesh. Our faith is solid in trusting the Lord. Secondly, we stand in the might of His power, not our own power. This armour must be worn to protect you from the wiles or trickery of the devil.

You do not fight against humans, but spirits with powers that work in the atmosphere or earthly realm. *Ephesians 2:2* "Wherein in time past ye walked according to the course of this world, according to the prince of the power of the air, the spirit that now worketh in the children of disobedience."

St. Matthew 8: 24-27

[24] And, behold, there arose a great tempest in the sea, insomuch that the ship was covered with the waves: but he was asleep.

[25] And his disciples came to him, and awoke him, saying, Lord, save us: we perish.

[26] And he saith unto them, Why are ye fearful, O ye of little faith? Then he arose, and rebuked the winds and the sea; and there was a great calm. [27] But the men

marveled, saying, What manner of man is this, that even the winds and the sea obey him!

So who was Jesus talking to? The water does not have ears. The wind does not have ears. He was talking to the spirit that was behind the storm. The devil was behind the storm, and he is behind the storms in your life. However, you should always remember that Jesus is on board.

Job 1:19 "And, behold, there came a great wind from the wilderness, and smote the four corners of the house, and it fell upon the young men, and they are all dead; and I only am escaped alone to tell thee." God allowed Satan to attack for a purpose, but he cannot do any more than God allows him to. He needed permission from God to do what he did. We know that the devil cannot control God, who has all power. God allows the enemy to work to fulfill His ultimate purpose.

The enemy works where a person is ignorant to the scripture. Fear comes where no knowledge of the word is present. Ignorance gives him the advantage. You must be girded about with truth; the Word must be rooted and grounded in your heart. You must speak truth at all times; you must believe the truth at all times. Whatever you face, you must put the truth before you and keep it there. If you tell a lie, you must tell another lie in order to cover up the first lie.

Truth stands all by itself; it does not need help to be true. The truth does not change, regardless of the circumstance. Truth will always win. *II John 1:4* "I rejoiced greatly that I found of thy children walking in truth, as we received a commandment from the Father."

The breastplate of righteousness is a vital part of your armour, it protects your heart from the evil arrows of the enemy. *Psalms 11:7* "For the righteous Lord loveth righteousness; his countenance doth behold the upright." The Lord blesses righteous people; not self righteousness, but His righteousness. **Proverbs 11: 6** "The righteousness of the upright shall deliver them: but transgressors shall be taken in their own naughtiness."

Proverbs 14: 34 "Righteousness exalted a nation: but sin is a reproach to any people."

You must have a right heart in order to do right. God will not work outside of His word. The helmet is to protect your mind from doubt and unbelief. You know you are saved. Your mind is fixed on believing that Jesus is the only way.

The sword of the Spirit is most needed to battle the enemy. Every soldier needs a weapon, and you must know how to use it. You must study it daily if you want to survive. *Romans 10:17* "So then faith cometh by hearing, and hearing by the word of God." Your heart must be full of the Word and full of faith. If a person feels like he or she is getting weak, the Word will make them strong again. Do not allow the enemy to make you think light of God's Word. It is what will save you from the enemy. Do not play around with the devil; you will never win in his ball park.

The devil does not play fair; he is a dirty fighter. Do not be like Samson. You'll find that women were his weakness. We must bring our weaknesses to the Lord. Samson loved Delilah but she was not in love with him. What you love can control you. You cannot play with the lust of the flesh, the lust of eyes, and the pride of life because they will destroy you. Many people are playing that same game today. Sin causes you to become weak. When you are weak, it is because you got out of the Word. The way to return to God is to get back into His Word. The Word causes you to grow spiritually.

To be strong in the power of His might means walking in the power of the Spirit. When Jesus was in the wilderness to be tempted of the devil, he fasted forty days and forty nights to give us an example. Remember fasting from time to time helps to keep the flesh under subjection. When Jesus came out of the wilderness from being tempted of the devil, he came out in the power of the Spirit. He was full of the Holy Ghost. He knew who He was. The devil did not have a chance in deceiving Him. You must follow His example if you want victory. The flesh is no weapon for spiritual warfare. You must have the Holy Spirit in order to win the fight.

The enemy seeks to get in high places because he can do the most the damage when he is in a high position. Lying preachers are the number one reason why a lot of people are deceived. That is why you must know God's Word for yourself. Satan uses your ignorance to his advantage. You must use Spiritual weapons and not carnal weapons to fight the enemy.

II Corinthians 10:4 "For the weapons of our warfare are not carnal. But mighty through God to the pulling down of strongholds."

Fight with the Word of God. The Word will pull down every stronghold that the enemy has on a child of God, but you must apply the Word to your life in order to pull down imaginations and everything that comes against you.

So many times Christians can be carnally minded and not realize it. You must be watchful that the carnal man does not creep back into your life. Paul had a problem with the Corinthian church because they were so carnal and not spiritual. Carnality causes envy, strife, and divisions. God wants his people to mature and become good soldiers in His army. Maturity is the key to having victory in your life. The Word of God is what causes you to grow, and live a victorious life through Jesus Christ. God did not intend for you to be a spiritual midget or stay a baby in His army. You are fighting an intelligent foe that has plenty of experience in causing man to fall.

All of his efforts and energy is aimed towards something that is appealing to the flesh. The victory is in trusting God and His armour that He has provided. No carnal armour will be sufficient for you. Just as David could not use the armour that King Saul provided when he went out to fight Goliath. He had to use what he knew worked. You must take the same attitude, with God's armour. It gives you confidence in God when you do it His way.

You get in trouble with the Lord when you lean to your own understanding and turn to the beggarly elements of this world. It leads to false security. God cannot help you when you trust in the things of this world. These worldly things will lead you astray. God cannot be glorified in your life when you follow after things that cannot bring about security, and these things cannot secure victory in your life. Victory over the flesh, the devil, and the world can only come when you do it God's way. The gospel of peace must be preached throughout the world. It is the good news that people need in this evil day. The gospel is what saves you from sin and self. Last but not least, the weapon of prayer which is the most important part of your armour. When you pray, you release God's power into your situation. Prayer also causes angels to fight in your defense. Without prayer, all of your knowledge and experience is powerless.

Daniel 10:12, 13 Speaks about Daniel seeking the Lord for understanding concerning the future of Israel. As he was praying and fasting for twenty one days, a demonic spirit hindered the answer from coming. So the Archangel, Michael, came to help Gabriel in the battle. If angels need help in fighting evil spirits, you as a child of God need God's angelic help as well. A soldier in God's army must pray always. Prayer gives you the power to endure hardness as a good soldier. You cannot win this battle alone. Luke 18: 1-8 "And he spake a parable unto them to this end, that men ought always to pray, and not to faint;"

[2]"Saying, There was in a city a judge, which feared not God, neither regarded man:"

[3]" And there was a widow in that city; and she came unto him, saying, Avenge me of mine adversary."

[4] "And he would not for a while ; but afterward he said within himself, Though I fear not God, nor regard man;"

[5] "Yet because this widow troubleth me, I will avenge her, lest by her continual coming she weary me."

[6] "And the Lord said, Hear what the unjust judge saith."

[7]" And shall not God avenge his own elect, which cry day and night unto him, though he bear long with them? I tell you that he will avenge them speedily. Nevertheless when the Son of man cometh, shall he find faith on earth?"

You must learn to pray without ceasing.

Do not faint in your praying. God has His own time and way of doing things. So do not give up on God's plan, and let go of your plans.

He longs to answer your prayers, but prayers must be prayed first in order for the Lord to answer them. You must be walking in the Spirit to learn how to pray and wait. Trust Him with all your heart, and you will not be disappointed in His answer. Trust God.

Prayer works wonders. Prayer changes things. Prayer will also change you, even if God does not change your circumstance. He will equip you for the task that is set before you. You must also intercede for other saints who are in battle with the enemy of their soul as well. There is a certain strength that comes when you pray for others. Acknowledge the

Lord in everything you do, and He will direct your ways. God's way is the best way. The flesh will always lead you down the wrong road. If you learn to acknowledge God in everything you do, God will direct your thoughts and your foot steps in His divine plan. His purpose is for you to have victory in every area of your spiritual life, as well as your natural life. God is concerned about the whole man. Go and be victorious in Jesus Christ. For you are more than a conqueror.

John Correa

Terranto Shetley

Rosalyn Wabi-Titi, Tamo Achu

Robson Mulumbo

Russel Kenneth Pier

Christianandace Brockmeyer

Solomon Baddoo

Blegovest Fartsov

Lisette Rivera

John David Rivera

Jodie Cardinale-Falcon

Lavon Hightower Lewis

Bethany Gromel

Other books that are in progress.

1. Faith on Trial

2. Developing an Intimate

Relationship with God

3. Faith Versus Fear

4. Are you Expecting Yet?

5. Prayer

6. Religion or Salvation?

Vinney green
Francis Scott Gusha
Bishop Sky Barda
Humphrey Kaushoni
Brooke Gardner
Sanja Mandir Shotley
Misty Amburg
DESiree Haudershelt
Russell Kneeland
Nathaniel Moore
Glenn Gromer
Seth Jodge
Renato Duarte

Eva Heuvg
Emmanuel Phir
Rachael Madsen
Mervis Phin
Sharon Phin
MSJoy Marie
Evanglist Banny
Veda Scott
Laurence Janet Phin

Chicha Luchembe
Dave Albert

Jessica Marie Brackett
Pastor L. Vasha Piemont
Dennis N. Cindy Michaud

Caroline Turato
Daniel Schottmann
Alston D-R · Oliver
Art Vaillancourt
Tim Perkins

Benjamin Michael Wadt
Brenda Lee
Rachael Ecches Michael

Blessings to you all!

God's Children

David Nyamuta
Cindy Doyle
Kaitlyn Michaud
Bryan James
Luhanga Musumadi'
Sarah Ann Harter
William Musy Chouloute
Christina Zegarra
Pastor Hendrix Nwmba

Lizzy Ngosa Sifaya
Samuel Coleman
Peggy Mwila Wina (Peres)
Jerome Sanford
John Kenny
Vanny V. Leon
Phil Meek
Darrell Stubbs
Tyrue McCoy
Joshua Harter

Budsly Edman
Charles Scott
Peter Bistis
Lynn Marrie Thelwell
Polishician Derrick Zulu
John Roy Chisanga
Tennyson Musyani;

Leonard Ward
Michaelle Tuttle
Prudence Farrow
Benson Kalomo
Michael stubbs
Dennis N mark Brooker
Jiltriu Saebo

Donna Privitera
Rene Rengbonkon Blessing to all Gods
Princealimoll Ann Children
Christopher Anderson Botts
Iliya Stetlanov Shterev
Patrick Kisunda
Brian Snell
Yosef Bamishewitz
Matthew Darcy Ward
Casey Lynn Bowden
Nelson Varghese Junior

Kristin and Dustin Dewitt
Kathlene George
Prosper Cheloka
Lossy Hasiyu
Samuel Dupp
Kathleen George
Florence Mwumba Manga
Asiana James Bande
Gershonn Puri
Benny Greaver
Rebecca Boyle
Roberto Bango

CPSIA information can be obtained at www.ICGtesting.com
Printed in the USA
LVOW06084811 1011

250007LV00001B/7/P

9 781613 797365